WITHDRAWN

ICE FISHING

BRIDGET HEOS

rosen publishing's
rosen central®

New York

To my uncles John and Jerry, who took me fishing

Published in 2012 by The Rosen Publishing Group, Inc.
29 East 21st Street, New York, NY 10010

First Edition

Library of Congress Cataloging-in-Publication Data

Heos, Bridget.
Ice fishing / Bridget Heos.—1st ed.
     p. cm.—(Fishing: tips & techniques)
Includes bibliographical references and index.
ISBN 978-1-4488-4600-9 (library binding)
ISBN 978-1-4488-4607-8 (pbk.)
ISBN 978-1-4488-4738-9 (6-pack)
1. Ice fishing—Juvenile literature. I. Title.
SH455.45.H46 2012
799.12'2—dc22

2010051937

Manufactured in Malaysia

CPSIA Compliance Information: Batch #S11YA: For further information, contact Rosen Publishing, New York, New York, at 1-800-237-9932.

CONTENTS

Water is a magical material. Unlike most substances, it expands when it freezes. For this reason, ice floats rather than sinks, and, where the winters are cold, fishermen can walk out to the fish they hope to catch. People have been doing this for thousands of years as a way of enduring harsh winters. But today, ice fishing is as much about fun as it is tradition. Where the winters are long, it provides a reason to brave the cold. And thanks to new technology, ice anglers are better equipped to find fish, making for more exciting outings.

First ice marks the start of ice fishing season in the northern states and Canada. It's when, overnight, the ice on a nearby pond or lake creaks and groans until it fuses together. The next morning, it is several inches thick—and clear as glass. After making sure it's strong enough to walk on (at least 4 to 5 inches [10 to 13 centimeters]), fishermen make their way from the shore to the weedy shallows, where fish feed on plankton, other fish, and, hopefully, bait.

The basic idea of ice fishing hasn't changed much through history. Native Americans used to chisel out holes in the ice, drop a homemade wooden fish into

Ice fishermen peer into the icy water at the Brainerd Jaycees Ice Fishing Extravaganza on Gull Lake in Brainerd, Minnesota, on January 26, 2008. They were competing with ten thousand participants for $150,000 in prizes.

the water, cover themselves with a blanket to illuminate the hole, and then wait for a fish to appear. Then they would spear the fish. They also used fishing lines attached to short sticks—similar to the jigs used today. That single-hole jigging tradition, which depended on knowledge of the lake and a little luck, continued until recently. Today, sonar aids fishermen in predicting good fishing spots—and power augers allow them to try their luck at several holes. With ice fishermen now as mobile as their summer counterparts, the sport is growing in popularity. But many traditions, such as spearfishing through an illuminated hole in the ice, remain.

Ice fishing culture varies slightly from place to place. In Minnesota, fishermen seek walleye. In Wisconsin, some people spear sturgeon, a giant prehistoric fish. Alaskans catch salmon. Northwestern fishermen try for trout. Other fishermen are happy with a bucketful of panfish. Whatever the catch of the day, many fishermen think fish taste best when caught in icy waters.

Whether you grew up ice fishing with your family or are new to hard water fishing altogether, this book will help you become a more efficient modern ice fishing angler.

CHAPTER 1

WHERE TO ICE FISH AND HOW TO BE SAFE

The Ice Belt is the zone roughly north of latitude 40° where, throughout the world, ponds, lakes, and even parts of rivers and oceans freeze several inches deep during winter. In North America, it includes Canada, Alaska, Idaho, Montana, Wyoming, North and South Dakota, Wisconsin, Michigan, New York, Vermont, New Hampshire, Maine, and parts of Massachusetts, Connecticut, New Jersey, Pennsylvania, Ohio, Indiana, Illinois, Iowa, Nebraska, Colorado, Utah, and Nevada. There are also pockets of icy waters in the mountains of other states, including New Mexico, Arizona, and California.

Perhaps the most popular ice fishing region is the Great Lakes. The Great Lakes themselves are too big to freeze, but some of the bays get good ice. More commonly, people fish on smaller lakes and ponds in the Great Lakes states.

Minnesota is home to the most ice anglers in America. There, 150,000 permanent ice houses are pulled onto the lake each year—about 5,000 on Mille Lacs alone. People typically fish for walleyes, which are large game fish, or smaller panfish, such as perch. Competitions like the Eelpout Festival on Leech Lake award anglers who catch the biggest or most fish.

Ice fishing is also extremely popular in Michigan and Wisconsin. Each year, three hundred thousand people go ice fishing in Michigan. Houghton Lake is the largest inland lake in the state. Every year, it is host to Tip-Up Town USA, a winter festival featuring ice fishing, and other cold-weather activities, such as a polar bear dip (where people run into the freezing water in their swimsuits). In Wisconsin, anglers fish for the usual game fish and panfish. But they also have a unique tradition: spearfishing for sturgeon, an ancient fish that can grow to 200 pounds (91 kilograms).

Many lakes in New York don't enjoy the thick ice of Minnesota, Wisconsin, or Michigan, but New Yorkers still have many ice fishing options. Lakes freeze over throughout the state, and the bays of Lake Ontario and Adirondack waters such as Lake Champlain and Lake George are especially beautiful. Here, anglers may even be able to score some salmon, a difficult hard water catch.

Permanent ice houses like this one on Gull Lake in Minnesota are rigged for heat and other creature comforts. However, if the fish aren't biting inside, fishermen must venture out.

Though New England is close to the shore, it receives long, cold winters because maritime winds (which are warmer than land winds) blow west to east—away from Maine, New Hampshire, and Massachusetts. The opposite is true of northwestern coastal states, such as Oregon and Washington, which have milder winters because of winds blowing in from the Pacific.

In Maine, winter is known as the time of year when locals take back the waterfront. Many wealthy people summer in Maine lake homes. But in the winter, ice anglers pull shanties onto the ice and have lakefront

Teen boys fish the lagoon at Sacajawea Park in Livingston, Montana, in 2005. For a quick fishing trip close to home, a spud, an auger, and jigging poles may be all you need.

property. Actually, it's better than lakefront property because they are literally on the lake. They're not trespassing because the Great Ponds Act states that lakes over 10 acres (.04 square kilometers) are public property. Most northern states have similar laws granting public rights to navigable waters.

On the opposite side of the Great Lake states, the Badlands and Black Hills of North and South Dakota offer trout fishing opportunities at Sheridan, Deerfield, and Pactola lakes. Because of Deerfield Lake's high elevation, anglers can often ice fish for a longer season than elsewhere in the state. The lake has rainbow and brook trout and splake (a mix between char and brook trout). The Dakotas also have some off-the-beaten-path lakes, which can only be accessed by skis or snowmobile.

Farther west, anglers can try their luck in the snow-fed lakes in the Rocky Mountains of Montana, Wyoming, Utah, and Colorado. Montana has some huge lakes that are good for ice fishing. Flathead Lake, the largest natural freshwater lake in the western United States, is too big to freeze, but its bays do. Fort Peck Lake, in northeast Montana, is 250,000 acres (1,011 square km) and 220 feet (67 meters) deep. It is home to more than fifty kinds of fish.

Ice fishing has become more popular in Colorado in recent years. The Department of Fish and Wildlife hatchery program now stocks lakes and reservoirs in late fall. That means many favorite Colorado fish, such as rainbow trout, brook trout, cutthroat trout, and kokanee salmon, are available in the winter, too. The best-known ice fishing lakes include Georgetown Lake, Eleven Mile Reservoir, Harvey Gap Reservoir, and Evergreen Lake in greater Denver.

Much farther west, Alaska is known for its salmon fishing—both in summer and winter. Salmon are so much a part of the culture that school-children learn about the lifecycles of salmon by ice fishing through the state's "Salmonids in the Classroom" program. Chinook and kokanee

DOLLY VARDEN TROUT
Adult female

Here is a drawing of the Dolly Varden trout. This type of fish averages between 1 and 4 pounds (.45 and 1.8 kg).

salmon are common fish caught through the ice, as well as Dolly Varden trout and arctic char.

Finally, there is Canada, where nearly the entire country is ice fishing territory. Like in Alaska, even parts of the ocean freeze, so you can ice fish on saltwater inlets. Quebec, for instance, has one of the largest saltwater ice fishing villages in the world: Pêche Blanche du Fjord. There, ice fishermen (and women) fish for redfish, cod, and rainbow smelt, among others. But ice fishing on lakes, such as Lake Nipissing and Lake Simcoe, is more common. Lake Simcoe, an hour north of Toronto, hosts the annual Canadian ice fishing championship and is considered the ice fishing capital of North America. Every winter, four thousand huts go up on the lake, where yellow perch is a popular catch.

Now that you know where to fish, let's talk about the single most important thing you need to know before getting there: safety.

Be Safe on the Ice

If you've ever watched the *Deadliest Catch*, you know that falling into frigid water is a big deal. Within minutes, you can lose consciousness— just because of the cold. Add a ceiling of ice to the equation, especially if you're in moving water, and you've got a very dangerous situation. That's why when it comes to ice fishing, preventing falls through the ice is the top priority.

Ice should be at least 4 to 5 inches (10 to 13 centimeters) deep just to walk on. If you are fishing with a group, it should be 7 inches (18 cm). For waters with heavy currents, such as rivers, make that 8 to 10 inches (20 to 25 cm). To drive a vehicle on ice, you'll need at least 18 inches (46 cm). Keep in mind that shock waves due to pressure from vehicles and natural elements like underwater springs and carp wallows can weaken the ice. Standard advice is to drive with windows down, doors unlocked, seatbelts off, and a hand on the door handle. But the truth is, survival rates are low for drivers that fall through the ice. Don't risk driving (or riding in a car) on thin ice.

As you walk out onto the lake, particularly during first and last ice, you should test the depth periodically by chiseling a hole and using a tape measure. Then tap the ice to test for hollowness. A hollow sound indicates that the water level has dropped. Ice isn't stable in this case because water isn't supporting it.

Once you determine that the ice is relatively safe, proceed with caution. Keep in mind that 4 inches (10 cm) in one spot can be 3 inches

A Vermont Fish & Wildlife game warden rescues Jodi, a Jack Russell terrier, on March 27, 2008. Her owner, an eighty-year-old man, had been fishing on Lake Champlain when his vehicle broke through the ice.

(8 cm) just a few feet away. Shore ice freezes first, so the ice might thin as you go farther out onto the lake. Pick at the ice in front of you with your spud (a long chisel) to feel for unstable spots. Continue to measure the depth as you go farther away from shore.

Because ice can vary and change, it's important to understand what affects ice thickness. First, there are geographical conditions. Bodies of water that are close to the ocean typically freeze later than those farther inland. The ocean stores heat from the summer sun. So the wind blowing off the relatively warm sea is warmer than wind blowing inland. With maritime winds typically blowing west to east, the Pacific Northwest and Europe get frozen waters at much higher latitude than elsewhere in the world. However, even New England lakes freeze later the closer they are to the ocean.

Next, there is the lake itself. Deep water and big water (which covers a large area) freeze later—if at all. Not only do large bodies of water retain heat better than smaller bodies of water, they also have stronger currents (moving water freezes at lower temperatures than still water) and blowing winds. For these reasons, the main bodies of the Great Lakes never freeze, though some bays and lagoons do. Likewise, the ocean freezes only around the poles. Rivers, which move very quickly, are also slower to freeze. Rivers pose an additional danger to ice fishermen. If you fall through the ice, you are swiftly carried downstream—away from the hole you drilled. Only venture out on an icy river with extreme caution.

A body of water also has features that can make the ice thinner in some places. This is especially true of large irregular lakes, which don't freeze uniformly. These features include underwater springs, creeks flowing into the lake, and patches of snow, which can insulate ice, making it warmer. Ice around objects frozen into the ice—such as boats or leaf piles—can also be unstable. Any lake in which the water level varies (such as those used for irrigation or power) should not be considered stable.

Other Safety Considerations

Aside from ice thickness, here are a few ice fishing safety considerations.

- **Hypothermia and frostbite**. Clothing will be discussed in the next chapter, but the main idea is to layer and be prepared. Be aware that windchill can make a 20°F (-7°C) day feel like a -22°F (-30°C) day. Getting wet, either from sweat or precipitation, will make you colder. Bring a dry set of clothes. Have hot liquids ready to drink. Also, know the lake and take extra care not to get lost in a storm.

- **Falls**. Avoid falls on slippery ice by wearing boots with good traction or creepers, which you can put over your boots for traction. When walking, keep your hands free to catch yourself. Cover sharp objects like auger blades when you move them to avoid injuries if you fall.

- **Fire safety and carbon monoxide concerns**. If you are in an icehouse with a heater, avoid carbon monoxide poisoning by having two sources of ventilation that are unclogged. For fire safety, don't lock icehouses from the inside.

Varying conditions include sunlight, wind, and other weather conditions. A shaded lake will freeze earlier than a sunny one. Lakes exposed to wind freeze later, particularly if the wind blows parallel to the lake, rather than perpendicularly. Early and late in the season, when the ice is at its thinnest, temperatures above freezing for six hours of the day can weaken the ice. Multiply the typical ice thickness needed by 1.3 to determine the ice thickness needed in this situation. For instance, instead of 4 to 5 inches (10 to 13 cm) of ice to walk safely, you would need 5.2 to 6.5 inches (13.2 to 16.5 cm). Temperatures above freezing (32°F [0°C]) for twenty-four hours or more mean that the ice is no longer safe, unless it is midwinter and the ice is very thick.

In spite of knowing the ice, accidents can happen. If you do fall through, don't panic. Face the direction you came from. Climb onto the ice. If that ice breaks, keep trying until you find stable ice. Once you are out of the water, do not stand. Instead, roll to land. Change into dry clothes, and seek medical attention.

If the person you are with falls through the ice, you'll need to help him or her without becoming a victim yourself. Don't run to the hole, as more ice could collapse. Instead, throw or extend an item to the friend, such as a rope, jumper cables, or skis. Once out of the water, get your friend into dry clothes. Seek medical help. Even if he or she feels fine, hypothermia can set in later.

CHAPTER 2

WHAT TO BRING: FROM BASIC TO HIGH-TECH EQUIPMENT

The next thing you need to get started is equipment. First, you'll need supplies to test the ice thickness: a chisel or spud and tape measure. Next, you'll need something to cut a larger hole in the ice. Technically, you could cut the hole with the same spud, but it's much easier to use an auger. An auger looks like a giant corkscrew. With a manual auger, you turn it through the ice yourself, which is labor-intensive, especially if the ice is very thick. Most people today use a power auger so that they can quickly drill multiple holes.

Power augers were introduced after World War II, but didn't become affordable, reliable, and lightweight until the mid-1980s. At that point, they helped revolutionize ice fishing. Now, people could quickly drill multiple

When power augers became lightweight and affordable, they revolutionized ice fishing. Now, several holes can be drilled in order to find the hot bite.

holes, rather than chiseling out one and hoping for the best. Today, holes are the equivalent of casts—you try several until you find the fish. Power augers come in various sizes. A 5-inch (around 13-cm) auger works for panfish, whereas 8 to 10 inches (20 to 25 cm) might be necessary for game fish. Deeper ice requires more horsepower. Power augers cost in the range of $200 to $600. The blades can be kept sharp with an India or Arkansas stone. To keep the hole clear once you drill, you'll need a simple tool called a skimmer.

Next, you'll need ice fishing rods—called jigging rods or jigs. (There are also open-water jigging rods—the term simply means the line is in the water beneath you, as opposed to being cast out into the water.) Like other modern fishing rods, ice rods are made of graphite or fiberglass. However, ice rods are shorter than standard fishing rods. This is because when your line goes straight down into the water and you need to muscle a fish out of a small hole, a long pole can be unwieldy. They vary in weight from ultra-light (for fishing panfish), to light (for fishing panfish or small game fish), to heavy (for game fish. A heavier rod can bring in a big fish, but a lighter rod allows you to move the lure more effectively and feel bites more acutely.

For light rods, a light reel is needed to achieve higher sensitivity—a necessity in winter, when the fish tend to bite less heartily. The spool doesn't have to be very long, since ice fishing doesn't require casting and you won't likely fish more than 20 to 50 feet

Lightweight jigging rods like this one are perfect for catching panfish, as they allow the fisherman to feel a light bite at the end of the line.

(6 to 15 m) deep. However, allow for some extra line in case the fish runs, and make sure the reel has good drag.

The fishing line should stand up under harsh weather. Monofilament or fluorocarbon is best. Match your test line to the fish you're trying to catch: panfish, 4 to 6 pound (2 to 3 kg) test line; trout, 6 pound (3 kg); pike and other game fish, 12 to 14 pound (5 to 6 kg). For bigger fish, you may need 20 to 80 pound (9 to 36 kg) test line with a steel leader.

Ice fishermen also use special fishing contraptions called tip-ups. These are like a fishing rod, only without the rod. They simply have a spool and line attached to a base. You set the tip-up directly over the hole. A flag goes up when you get a bite. Then you set the tip-up aside and pull the line up by hand. You can buy handcrafted wooden tip-ups or manufactured polar tip-ups. Most places have limits on the number of tip-ups you can use—such as four per fisherman.

Generally, you use bait for tip-ups and lures for jigs (perhaps tipped with bait). This is because you can move your jig, making the lure move according to its design. But tip-ups are left alone in the water, so the movement of the minnow or other live bait is needed to attract the fish. Allow your live bait to move naturally by hooking it the right way. Minnows should be hooked through their backs, for instance. For worms, it's a good idea to hook one all the way through and then tip the hook with a squirming live worm.

Different lures and bait work for different situations. In general, clear water calls for natural-looking lures, whereas dark water requires flashier—even phosphorescent—lures. Small lures work for panfish, whereas big lures—3 to 6 inches (8 to 15 cm)—are better for game fish. It's also best to match the lure to the fish's natural food. If the fish

"Jig" also refers to a lure attached to a jig. This handmade airplane ice fishing jig is designed to catch lake trout. A good lure will resemble a smaller, and tasty-looking, fish.

eats plankton, small lures are best. If the fish eats fish, the lure should resemble fish. Moving lures, such as spinners, are best.

As far as bait, game fish like large minnows or golden shiners, whereas panfish like larvae or small minnows. For dark waters, you can now buy euro larvae, which are live bait dyed bright colors. Larvae can be kept warm by keeping them in a container in your pocket. You can keep minnows from freezing in the bucket by using a small aerator for the water.

Hook size varies according to fish size, but also according to the size of the fish's mouth. A treble hook is good for keepers, but can injure fish you intend to set free. If you intend to keep the fish, you'll want to bring a gaff (a handled hook for lifting heavier fish). Once the fish is close to the hole, you can hook it with the gaff and pull it through the hole. But if you're going to release the fish, the gaff may hurt it. You'll need to pull the fish in with your bare hands instead.

Bobbers can be used to show when you get a bite and measure your depth (if you know where the fish are, you can keep dropping your line to that spot). Other supplies you'll need include tools for cutting the line or making minor repairs, 5-gallon (19-liter) buckets for supplies and bringing home fish, nets for getting bait out of the bucket, and something to transport everything. This can be as simple as a child's sled or a homemade sled box, or as high tech as an ice fishing container that doubles as a portable shelter. You can pull them by hand, or with a snow mobile or ATV, or, on very thick ice, a truck.

Creature Comforts and High-Tech Gear

The St. Paul Ice Fishing Show is the largest in the United States and attracts thousands of shoppers. Here, you can find some of the most innovative ice fishing supplies in the world. These include the portable ice shelter.

On very cold days, a shelter allows anglers to brave the elements. In the past, permanent shelters were moved on and off the lake once a year. They were too heavy to move more often than that. If the fish weren't biting beneath the shelter, there wasn't much you could do. With the invention of the portable shelter, however, fishermen can now

Neal Thomas *(left)* and Luke Chase head for the weigh-in station at the Brainerd Jaycees Ice Fishing Extravaganza on January 21, 2006, in Brainerd, Minnesota.

drill some holes, see where the fish are biting, and set up the shelter there. It's lightweight and easy to set up and take down.

Some people still opt for permanent shelters, however, perhaps because they provide a sense of home. You can paint it a bright color, put in a well-ventilated propane or wood-burning stove, add some creature comforts, and, voilà, you have a lake home. If it's atop a honey hole, you can actually fish there. If not, it can serve as home base. Most ice shelters are pretty bare-bones—a beadboard serves as insulation; windows, if required, are cut out; and a table and chairs create a dinner spot. However, there are some luxury models. One was featured in the Neiman Marcus Christmas catalog with a price tag of $27,000!

Dave Genz: Fish Trapper

Dave Genz is considered the father of modern ice fishing. He pioneered the mobile, flexible style of ice fishing that is used today. He also created jigs that catch heavy fish for their size and the first instant-setup portable ice shelter. Genz came from a family of ice fishermen. His dad, a construction engineer with time off in the winter, fished Mille Lacs in Minnesota. Genz followed in his footsteps. As a maintenance engineer for American Linens, Genz was welding together a portable fish house one day when an engineer asked, "What is that?" Genz said it was a Fish Trap, and that's how it got its name.

Even with a shelter, you'll need to dress warmly. Layers are key. Specifically, you'll want the first layer to wick away sweat and other moisture, the second to warm you, and the third to block the wind. If it's snowing, you might also want a waterproof shell. These items can be found at most outdoor clothing stores. There is also gear specific to ice fishing, including clothes with big zips (so that you can shed layers when your fingers are numb), pants with knee pads, neoprene gloves that stay warm when wet, and boots rated to -150°F (-101°C). These items are great for midwinter trips; on warmer days, a hoodie might suffice. You'll always need plenty of gloves, especially if you are wrestling big fish out of the hole. Bring several pairs in a Ziploc bag.

Another important creature comfort is warm food. Fried fish fillets and potatoes are a typical shore lunch. You can deep-fry the fish and potatoes with a fish cooker, or simply fry them in a pan over a wood or gas stove. You may also want to bring stuff to do—skates, snowshoes, a football—anything to stay moving and keep warm. However, if you, or the people nearby, are serious about fishing, don't make a lot of ruckus. It scares off the fish.

Finally, for ice anglers willing to invest extra money in the catch of the day, there are several gadgets that help locate fish. These include a depth finder, which is helpful because fish often feed in shallows or at drop-offs. To use a depth finder, which looks like a flashlight, you clear away snow and set the unit directly on the ice. The depth finder tells you the water depth. For more information about the bottom of the lake, you can buy a special fishing GPS. This is like a regular GPS, only it allows you to download contour maps, which show underwater features like drop-offs, shoals, and sunken islands. Finally, fish finders allow you to see where the actual fish are. Fish show up as lines or colors on the screen, allowing you to lower your lines to the correct depth and revise your presentation if the fish are there but not biting. Fish finders range in price from less than $100 to several thousand dollars. Nowadays, you can even purchase an underwater camera and view the fish you're trying to catch as if it's on television!

Many of these gadgets are expensive. Keep in mind that they are a luxury—not a necessity for ice anglers. Ice fishing is known as a relatively cheap outdoorsman sport. Less high-tech methods of finding fish include studying a lake map, searching for weeds that have drifted to the surface, or talking to bait shop workers and other anglers. Remember, thousands of years ago, people fished with nothing but a spear and blanket—and they counted on their success to feed their families.

CHAPTER 3

How to Ice Fish:
The Basics

The first step of any ice fishing trip is to know the parameters. Rules and regulations vary from place to place, but typical ones include:

- Having a fishing license.
- Fishing during a certain season.
- Limiting your number of tip-ups.
- Using only certain lures, hooks, and bait. (Some states don't allow nonindigenous species as bait, for instance.)
- Catching a limited number, size, or species of fish.
- Following icehouse rules about locks, windows, ventilation, and the date it needs to be removed.

There are also environmental considerations. These include keeping the lake clean and well balanced.

Fishermen head off the ice after the Brainerd Jaycees Ice Fishing Extravaganza, the world's largest ice fishing competition. They tote their gear in a sled, an essential piece of ice fishing equipment.

Be sure to pick up trash before it blows into the lake. Also, plan to throw back fish that you won't eat—and large fish that are needed to maintain the population. In the winter, catch-and-release can be tricky. If fish fall on the ice, they can suffer from freeze burn. Even handling them too much can remove their slimy layer, which protects them from infection. Finally, the hook itself can damage the mouth, decreasing their ability to survive in the wild.

If you plan to recycle fish, pull in the fish gently—with your hands, not a gaff. Keep the fish off the ground. Carefully remove the hook, and get it back in the water as soon as possible. You will probably have time to snap a picture, but not enough time to carry it around the lake for a victory lap. Set it in the water head first, and hold it there for a minute. It will be tired (like how we feel after holding our breath). Once it is moving again, you can gently release it.

Tragedy on the Ice

On March 2, 2010, Jocelyn Belanger drove his truck onto about 1 foot (30 cm) of ice on the Ottawa River in Canada in order to retrieve an icehouse with a friend. As they hooked up the last house, the back wheel of Belanger's truck sunk into the ice. A friend was going to tow him out. Both men got under their trucks to hook up the tow. At that point, Belanger's truck crashed through the ice, taking Belanger with it. His friend reached into the icy water, trying to save him, but Belanger was swept away by the strong river current. He was later found dead. This tragic story shows both the danger of driving a vehicle onto the ice and of breaking through the ice on a river.

The next step to ice fishing is to know your lake. Get a map with contours and find out where the structures—or features—are. Structures or features are parts of the lake that aren't uniform. An example is weeds or rubble at the bottom, as opposed to the mud or sand that covers the rest of the lake. (Some people sink old trees or shrubs in strategic places before the lake freezes to create fish-attracting structures.) Another example is a drop-off leading from shallow to deep water.

Next, talk to fishery departments, bait shop workers, and other anglers. Different lakes are known for different fish. For instance, in Michigan, Saginaw Bay is known for its walleyes; Hamlin for perch; Higgins for smelt. There is even a part of Higgins Lake known as Smeltville, where fishermen seek this small but tasty fish. There are also several online message boards where you can find out what is biting where. But don't be afraid to try your own spot based on an

David Loope walks on Oneida Lake in New York, where the ice was 8 to 10 inches (20 to 25 cm) deep. First ice can be as clear as glass. With time, it turns white.

educated guess. Have a game plan for places you want to fish, but be flexible.

Fish follow both seasonal and daily migration patterns. Early in the ice fishing season, panfish start out in weedy shallows, about 15 feet (4.6 m) deep, in search of food. Later in winter, they retreat to deep water flats—about 30 feet (9 m) down. At this point, they hang out at drop-offs or near midlake structures, such as sunken islands. They return to shallows to feed—but not as far into the shallows. In late ice, they return more frequently and go farther into the shallows.

No matter the time of year, fish tend to move daily from deeper water structures to shallow water to feed. This route may be along a weed line or structure such as a reef. It may also be along a sharply sloping shore, which makes for a quick route. There might be a holding area along the route, where they'll find food or cover. This might be the first break line between shallow and deep water, or, in poor conditions, the second break line.

Game fish hunt panfish, so they tend to be where the panfish are, only slightly deeper. Both panfish and game fish hide out around structures, which include reefs, stone walls, sunken bars, sunken islands, points, and lagoons. Combination structures, such as weeds and rubble, are especially attractive to fish. If you have sonar, you can use it to further pinpoint lake features—and where the fish are. If you find a hot spot, use your GPS to record the coordinates. It will probably be a good fishing hole on other days, too.

In addition to migrating, fish tend to bite more zealously at certain times of the day and certain parts of the season. Winter fish generally feed at the same time as they do in the summer, so a dusk-and-dawn summer fish is also a dusk-and-dawn winter fish. Season-wise, early ice and late ice are known to be good times to fish.

First ice is what people call ice when a body of water first freezes over. If it hasn't snowed, the ice is also called black ice. Black ice looks

Tip-ups like this one on Lake Willoughby in Vermont can be used to test several areas for fish and attract fish through the use of multiple baits.

like glass. First ice may creak and groan—but not because you are walking on it. That is just the sound of ice fusing. It may also have natural cracks, which formed when the ice fused. These can actually help you gauge the depth of the ice. Know the difference between a dangerous sound (that of ice breaking) and a normal sound (of ice fusing), and between a dangerous crack and a crack that is natural this time of year. You have to be especially careful at first ice because the thickness may vary. As the season progresses, the ice will turn to white marble ice. Eventually snow will cover the ice.

Late ice occurs in the spring. Rescues are especially common in the spring, as warmer days weaken the ice in some places. While ice is thickest by the shore during first ice, it is weakest by the shore during late ice.

Weather-wise, light snow is considered good for fishing, whereas fish tend to hide during heavy snowfalls. Warm fronts are considered good; cold fronts, bad. Stable weather is good. For all these fishing beliefs, you'll find that the best time to catch fish is...whenever you catch fish. Nobody understands all the variables, and it's important to keep an open mind and always put safety first.

The Basics of Tip-ups and Jigs

The beauty of tip-ups is that you can set them up in various holes, and when you find a hot spot, move the other tip-ups nearby. Also, if you're with a group, all those baits tend to attract schools of panfish. If, on the other hand, fish are spooked by a large crowd, at a tournament for instance,

This angler uses pliers to remove a hook from a pike's mouth before releasing him back into the water. You must be careful not to hurt the fish when removing the hook.

you may want to set tip-ups on the quieter side of the lake in hopes that the fish will flee from the crowd to you. For fish that are easily spooked, you may even want to watch the tip-ups from shore, rather than on the ice.

The key to tip-up success is to focus on one type of fish. Cater your hook, line, and bait to that fish. Don't go for a trophy pike and some little fryers for dinner. You'll end up with neither. At the same time, be open-minded. A walleye presentation may result in an eelpout catch. If you have your heart set on fish for dinner, it's time to learn how to cook eelpout! When your flag goes up, pull the line in slowly by hand. Jerking it can cause you to lose the fish.

Although tip-ups allow you to have more lines on the ice, you will likely catch more fish by jigging. You're better equipped to move the hook to different levels and to make the lure move. In the winter, slighter motions are better because fish don't work as hard for their food. For this same reason, bites may be light. Hold the line or use a bobber to detect the slightest hits.

The jig rod needs to be short so that you can muscle the fish out of the hole. For panfish, 18 to 26 inches (46 to 66 cm) is a good size, whereas you may need a 36 to 42 inch (91 to 107-cm) rod for game fish. Midsize fish will require something in between. Cater the lure to the species—light-tipped for panfish, bigger and with more action for game fish. When you catch the fish, there are two schools of thought: Hook it while it runs, or wait till it stops. The latter is the point when the fish eats the bait, so the hook should be firmly in its mouth. Tug the line to place the hook. Then reel it in. When the fish is at the hole, you may have to pull it out by hand. If you plan to eat the fish, a gaff will help. If you plan to return it, use your hands. As you can imagine, your hands will get cold. After the big catch, a heater comes in handy!

If you do catch fish, remember your location. It may be a honey hole—a spot you can return to for consistent action.

How to Fillet a Fish of Any Size

There are two basic ways to clean a fish. One way is to remove the head, skin, and guts, leaving the skeleton and meat intact. In this case, after you cook and eat the fish, you're left with a comb on your plate. The other method is to fillet the fish and cook the boneless meat. Here is how to do the latter. Be sure to work with caution!

1. Lay the fish on its side. Carefully cut along the "neckline" of the fish from the fin at the side of its head along the gill and to the top of the head. This will be an angled cut.

2. Cut along the side of the backbone that is facing up. When near the head, do not cut too deep. As you get closer to the tail, and you no longer feel ribs, you can cut all the way through until you reach the tail.

3. Lift up the fish meat along the backbone and scrape your knife along the rib cage until all the meat is removed from the ribs. At this point, the fillet should be completely removed from the fish.

4. Flip the fillet over skin side down. Work your knife between the skin and the meat until the skin is removed.

5. Repeat on the other side. You'll be left with two boneless fillets and the fish skeleton—with guts intact, which can be discarded.

CHAPTER 4

HOW TO CATCH PANFISH AND GAME FISH

ce fishing boils down to two categories of fish: panfish and game fish. A whole panfish can typically fit in a pan—hence the name. There are some trophy panfish that are much bigger. For instance, the world record for yellow perch (a popular ice fishing panfish) is 4 pounds, 3.5 ounces (around 2 kg). But that was set in 1865! More commonly, yellow perch are 3 to 11 inches (8 to 28 cm) and just 4.8 to 10.88 ounces (136 to 308 grams). Because of the small-medium size, panfish feed on plankton and very small fish and get eaten by bigger fish.

Panfish

Panfish are the most common target of ice fishermen. And it's no wonder. Panfish are plentiful in most waters, including rivers, backwaters, ponds, lakes,

These colorful perch belong to David Smith, who was competing at the Rifle Gap Ice Fishing Tournament in Colorado on January 21, 2006.

and bays. They are prolific breeders. If their numbers exceed their food supply, they're easy to catch but small and of poor quality. At a more balanced lake, they're less plentiful but a better quality.

Below are tips for catching specific types of panfish.

Bluegill

This member of the sunfish family prefers to feed in the late afternoon and evening. They're enthusiastic biters, so if you find them, you'll catch them. They eat plankton, so your lures should be small—even flies work well. For bait, they like wax worms or mousie grubs.

Crappies

Crappies are also a kind of sunfish and one of the most commonly caught fish in the North Country, with the black crappie being more common than the white (though they look a lot alike). Crappies are generally found in shallow water from just under the ice to the tops of weeds. In clear water, they go deeper. Sometimes, they school in open water, too. The best time to catch them is from

An angler shows off a small, freshly caught bluegill. The largest bluegill ever caught in the United States weighed more than 4 pounds (1.8 kg).

two hours after dark until around 10 PM. If you're able to tell where the crappies are, lower your bait to above their eye level, as their eyes are positioned for upfeeding. Jig for them with a medium-sized minnow on a double hook, and give them plenty of line, as resistance causes them to drop the bait. You'll be glad if the crappies are biting. They taste great!

Yellow Perch

Yellow perch are found everywhere. They're a good fish to seek when you're making a day of ice fishing because they feed during daylight. Because their schools number fifty to two hundred fish, you can catch a lot in a short time. While they school with like-sized fish, you might find larger perch on the outer edge of the school. Within their body of water, they like channels, rocky points, and drop-offs—they can be found up to 40 feet (12 m) deep! They're likely to stay put for days, so ask other fishermen where they are biting. Perch eat small fish, so use a minnow as bait or a 1.5-inch (4-cm) Swedish pimple or other swimming lure.

White Perch

This "perch" is really a bass. It's not called a white bass because another bass is already named that. In fact, the two species sometimes mate, creating a hybrid. Native to Quebec, New England, and New York, the white perch has invaded the Great Lakes, threatening the walleye population by eating its eggs. White perch are good to eat, and if you fish for them in the Great Lakes, you'll be doing your part to save the walleyes. White perch can be caught at dusk along muck-bottom flats 15 to 30 feet (4.6 to 9 m) deep. Small minnows work well as bait.

Stocked Trout

Alpine lakes and mountain reservoirs are home to trophy trout—so you might want to fish for them as you would for game fish, with heavier lines and bigger bait. But stocked trout are often smaller. You can check with your state or local fisheries department for information on which lakes are stocked with trout. Trout feed during the early morning, at twilight, and on gloomy days. A spinning lure tipped with bait works well, and for bait, they like wax worms, night crawlers, minnows, and shrimp.

Kokanee Salmon

Most salmon species are considered game fish, but kokanee salmon are smaller. Don't let their size fool you though: They fight hard when caught—and they're hard to catch. Typically found in the western United States and the high country, kokanee can best be caught with a light line, small hook, and small bait or Swedish pimple.

Smelt

Perhaps it doesn't have the best name for a fish, but smelt is tasty. So much so

44

Rudy Manzanunez ice fishes in Belmont Harbor, on Lake Michigan, on January 29, 2004. In the background is downtown Chicago. Ice fishing is not a sport that takes place only in rural areas.

that even though it's small enough to be used as bait, smelt is still the most popular catch at some lakes, including Lake Champlain and Lake George. Smelt usually congregate in the same places each year, so talking to other fishermen is helpful. However, invasive species

This walleye, caught at the Brainerd Jaycees Ice Fishing Extravaganza, was weighed and then released, which is true of all fish caught at the tournament.

and changing lakes can force smelt into new habitats, which has happened at Lake Champlain. Traditionally, fishermen use a large diameter spool nailed to a wall of an ice shack to catch smelt. The presentation is similar to what you'd use to catch yellow perch. A bobber indicates when you have a bite. Then the line is reeled in by hand. You can also jig for smelt.

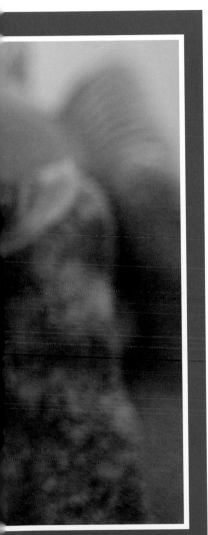

Game Fish

Game fish eat panfish, and so they are often found where panfish are found. However, you need a heavier line, bigger hook, and bigger bait to catch game fish, so you can't kill two birds with one stone (or, rather, two types of fish with one rod). Another difference is that while you can find good panfish in a small but well-balanced body of water, game fish in these places tend to be small and of poor quality. If you want to catch big fish, you should go to big water.

Popular winter game fish are northern pike, walleye, trout, salmon, and whitefish. Here are tips for catching each species.

Walleye and Sauger

Nicknamed "Old Glassy," the walleye is the sweet-heart of the ice fishing world. It is the state fish of Minnesota, where anglers bring home 3.5 million walleyes for a total of 4 million pounds (1,814,369 kg) every year. Regulations limit the number and size of walleyes that can be kept, so many are released. The walleye's popularity is no mystery. It provides thick white filets and presents a challenge to anglers. Sauger is similar to walleye but smaller and less common. Both fish can be caught using similar methods.

Walleye hold in deep dark water by day and feed in shallows at twilight and night. The best place to catch them is around irregular features that lead from the shallows to deep water. A submerged bar is an example of a popular walleye feature. Walleye fishing requires patience. A few days of no feeding will be followed by a bite, so don't give up.

As with all game fish, jigging is a good way to find walleyes. However, a tip-up with a minnow next to your jigging hole may attract the walleye to your jig pole, on which you can use a minnow-imitating lure. The walleye is a wary fish, so a light line—6-pound (3-kg) test—is necessary. Slowly lower and raise the line. When you hook the fish, pull it up steadily, giving it line when it runs. This is especially necessary near the hole, where most walleye are lost.

Many anglers fish for walleye on big rivers, such as the Fox, Wisconsin, Wolf, Mississippi, Rainy, and Saginaw. Backwaters and locks adjoining dams are especially good. As we've said in previous chapters, be especially cautious when ice fishing on rivers.

Eelpout

Anglers often catch eelpout when they're seeking walleye, so the fish is seen as a disappointment. It's true that eelpout are rather ugly. But most people don't catch fish for their looks but for their taste, and eelpout can be delicious. Here is how to catch the fish also known as burbot, freshwater cod, lawyer, and poor man's lobster.

On the Hunt for Sturgeon

Spearfishing is legal in seven states: Minnesota, Wisconsin, Michigan, North Dakota, South Dakota, Montana, and Alaska. Native American tribes regulate their own hunting and fishing. However, only Lake Winnebago and its tributaries in Wisconsin allow sturgeon spearfishing.

This involves cutting a large rectangular hole and covering it with a dark house (a windowless icehouse) or a blanket. This causes the light from the lake to shine through the hole (just as you can see through a window at night from inside a dark room). The fisherman drops a decoy tied to a string into the water. When the sturgeon (which can grow to 200 pounds [91 kg]) approaches the decoy, a spear is thrown at it. Sturgeon season is over after a certain number are caught (around one thousand to two thousand), which protects the prehistoric fish.

Early ice is the time period just before eelpout spawn. At this time, they can be found in the shallow structural features of the main lake. They go deeper later in the season—they've been caught as deep as 700 feet (213 m). For this reason, they're often found in deep waters such as the Great Lakes. Your best bet is to arrive in the afternoon to drill various holes along a steep-breaking structure that you think eelpout will follow. Just after dark, the fish will begin to move along the structure and hopefully bite.

Rocker-style lures tipped with minnows work well on tip-ups. For your jig pole, use a glow-in-the-dark jig head and live bait. Eelpout bait

An ice fisherman from northern Michigan holds up the pike he just caught using a tip-up. Before using a tip-up, make sure that it is legal in your area.

needs to be fresh, so change it about every fifteen minutes. Because it's nighttime, you can use a heavy line without spooking the eelpout. You should hold the line just off the bottom. When you catch an eelpout, be prepared for it to dive deeper as it fights for freedom.

Pike

Known as the Great White of the North, pike is the top predator of northern lakes and can grow from 2 to 30 pounds (.9 to 14 kg). It feeds from sunup to noon, lurking in weed beds just 7 to 16 feet (2 to 5 m) deep. Live bait on a jig works best, and heavy line is necessary. When you hook one, you may have to let it run several times as it approaches the hole. Finally, you should be able to grab it by the gills and pull it in. Watch out, though—they have sharp teeth!

Smallmouth and Largemouth Bass

Bass like oxygenated water, so first and last ice and water around springs are good places to look. (You can use a temperature probe to find springs, which are warmer than the rest of the water. For this reason, be careful of weak ice around the spring.) Bass are known to be picky eaters in the winter, so use their favorite bait: golden shiners for largemouth bass and crawdads for smallmouths.

Lake Trout

Native to northern America and Canada, lake trout like cold water and live in deep lakes such as Lake Superior and mine pits in the Canada Shield. In the summer, they go very deep, where the water is colder. But in winter, all depths are cold, so they can be found at

Joe Boutell *(left)* and Colin Venn catch a brown trout through a hole in the ice on December 10, 2008, in Racine, Wisconsin. They later released the fish.

mid-depth—20 to 50 feet (6 to 15 m) deep. They are often found alone instead of in schools. It's a good idea to paint your hook and lure a phosphorescent orange, and use a sucker or chub for bait.

Brown Trout

Brown trout is a beautiful fish that is native to Germany but was introduced to American waters. It's typically 12 to 22 inches (30–56 cm) when caught. They bite from dawn to 8 AM, and a medium pond shiner or minnow is good bait.

Salmon

Catching winter salmon is rare along the southern edge of the Ice Belt because they need very cold and very oxygenated water. Such waters, like the deep parts of the Great Lakes, seldom freeze. However, farther north in places such as Alaska, salmon are one of the primary species to ice fish. Salmon can be big and strong, so use a heavy line, 12 to 17 pounds (5 to 8 kg), and a swimming lure tipped with a minnow. When you hook a salmon, be prepared for it to fight for up to an hour before it lets you pull it from the hole.

GLOSSARY

angler A person who uses a hook and line to catch fish.

auger A large corkscrew apparatus turned either manually or through gas power to cut holes in ice.

bait Food, such as a fish or insect, put on a hook to catch a fish.

bay Part of an ocean, sea, or lake that cuts into the shoreline and is partially enclosed by land.

big water Water that covers a large area.

carbon monoxide An odorless, colorless, and tasteless gas that is highly toxic to humans.

darkhouse spearing A type of spearfishing in which the fisherman is in a windowless shelter and is thus able to see the illuminated water beneath the ice.

feature In fishing, a part of the lake that is different from the rest of the lake and attracts fish. It could be an underwater wall, a sudden change of depth, or a bed of weeds.

fillet A boneless piece of fish; the act of deboning a fish to prepare it for cooking.

frostbite Tissue damage—sometimes permanent—caused by exposure to cold.

gaff A large hook used to pull a fish out of the water.

game fish Those species at the top of the food chain that tend to be larger than a pan.

GPS (global positioning system) A navigation system that shows people where they are in relation to satellite-based maps.

hard water Another name for ice.

hypothermia Lowered body temperature that can be caused by exposure to cold and can lead to health emergencies.

Ice Belt The part of the world, generally above latitude 40°, where inland water freezes hard in the winter.

icehouse A temporary shelter in which anglers fish atop frozen bodies of water.

jig A lure that moves in the water by way of the fisherman moving the pole. A jig also refers to the pole itself and the act of fishing with this type of pole.

larvae The immature, worm-looking young of some insects.

latitude The angular distance, north and south, from the equator.

lure A nonfood object placed at the end of a fishing line to attract fish.

panfish A species of fish that typically fit in a pan and are in the middle of the food chain.

permanent shelter A shelter pulled onto the ice to remain stationary throughout winter.

portable shelter A shelter easily moved from place to place on the ice.

presentation In fishing, any combination of line, hook, lure, and bait that is visible to fish.

shore lunch A meal eaten next to water or on top of frozen water, often consisting of fish and potatoes.

snowshoes Footwear used to walk on top of the snow.

tip-up A fishing contraption that includes a reel, line, and flag, and is set over a hole in the ice.

FOR MORE INFORMATION

Alaska Department of Fish and Game
ADF&G Headquarters
1255 West 8th Street
P.O. Box 115526
Juneau, AK 99811-5526
Web site: http://www.adfg.state.ak.us
(907) 465-4180
The Alaska Department of Fish and Game regulates fishing and offers
    information.

American Sportfishing Association
225 Reinekers Lane, Suite 420
Alexandria, VA 22314
Web site: http://www.asafishing.org
(703) 519-9691
The American Sportfishing Association represents the interest of
    sportsfishermen and the sportsfishing business.

Lake Simcoe Region Conservation Authority
120 Bayview Parkway, Box 282
Newmarket, ON L3Y 4X1
Canada
Web site: http://www.lsrca.on.ca
(905) 895-1281
The Lake Simcoe Region Conservation Authority works to conserve
    this large Canadian lake.

Minnesota Department of Natural Resources
500 Lafayette Road
St. Paul, MN 55155-4040

Web site: http://www.dnr.state.mn.us/fishing

(651) 296-6157

The Minnesota Department of Natural Resources regulates and offers
information about fishing in the state.

Wisconsin Department of Natural Resources

101 South Webster Street

P.O. Box 7921

Madison, WI 53707-7921

Web site: http://dnr.wi.gov/fish

(608) 266-2621

The Wisconsin Department of Natural Resources regulates fishing in
the state, handles fishing licenses, and offers fishing reports.

Web Sites

Due to the changing nature of Internet links, Rosen Publishing has
developed an online list of Web sites related to the subject of this book.
This site is updated regularly. Please use this link to access the list:

http://www.rosenlinks.com/fish/ice

For Further Reading

Allard, Tim. *Ice Fishing: The Ultimate Guide*. Ontario, Canada: Heliconia Press, 2010.

Genz, Dave, Al Lindner, and Doug Stange. *Ice Fishing Secrets*. New York, NY: In-Fisherman, 1991.

Leitch, Jay. *Darkhouse Spearfishing Across North America*. Fargo, ND: North Dakota State University, 2001.

Nesper, Larry. *The Walleye War: The Struggle for Ojibwe Spearing and Treaty Rights*. Lincoln, NE: University of Nebraska Press, 2002.

Nordin, Hans. *Ice Fishing* (Complete Guide to Ice Fishing). Broomall, PA: Mason Crest, 2002.

Nordstrom, Kathryn. *The Fish House Book*. Duluth, MN: Dovetailed Press, 2007.

Philpott, Lindsey. *Complete Book of Fishing Knots, Lines, and Leaders*. New York, NY: Skyhorse Publishing, 2008.

Salas, Laura Purdie. *Ice Fishing*. Mankato, MN: Capstone Press, 2007.

Baichtal, John. "Art Shanties Bring Art to the Lake." *Wired*, January 9, 2009. Retrieved September 12, 2010 (http://www.wired.com/geekdad/2009/01/art-shanties-br).

Berkhahn, Patti. "Ice Fishing for the First Time." Retrieved September 8, 2010 (http://www.wildlifenews.alaska.gov/index.cfm?adfg=wildlife_news.view_article&articles_id=191&issue_id=35).

Black Hills Badlands & Lake Association. "Ice Fishing." Retrieved September 8, 2010 (http://www.blackhillsbadlands.com/home/thingstodo/outdoorrecreation/winterfun/icefishing).

Breining, Greg. *A Hard-Water World: Ice Fishing and Why We Do It*. St. Paul, MN: Minnesota Historical Society Press, 2008.

Capossela, Jim. *Ice Fishing: A Complete Guide, Basic to Advanced*. Woodstock, VT: The Countryman Press, 1992.

CBC News. "Ottowa River Ice Tested Before Drowning." March 3, 2010. Retrieved October 3, 2010 (http://www.cbc.ca/canada/ottawa/story/2010/03/03/ottawa-louise-beaudry-jocelyn-belanger-drowning-ice.html).

Colorado Division of Wildlife. "Ice Fishing." Retrieved September 8, 2010 (http://wildlife.state.co.us/Fishing/Reports/IceFishing).

Colorado Tourism Office. "Avid Anglers: Ice Fishing in Colorado." Retrieved September 8, 2010 (http://www.colorado.com/Articles.aspx?aid=42358).

David, Isaiah. "Safety Tips for Ice Fishing in Alaska." *USA Today*. Retrieved September 10, 2010 (http://traveltips.usatoday.com/safety-tips-ice-fishing-alaska-4620.html).

Durham, Jason. *Ice Fishing* (Pro Tactics). Guilford, CT: Lyons Press, 2009.

Genz, Dave. "Clam Ice Fishing." Retrieved September 12, 2010 (http://www.clamcorp.com/ProStaff/DaveGenz/tabid/332/Default.aspx).

About the Author

Bridget Heos is the author of several young adult nonfiction titles on topics ranging from biographies to science to states. Prior to being an author for teens, she was a newspaper reporter and freelance journalist. She lives in Kansas City with her husband and three sons.

About the Consultant

Contributor Benjamin Cowan has more than twenty years of both freshwater and saltwater angling experience. In addition to being an avid outdoorsman, Cowan is a member of many conservation organizations. He currently resides in western Tennessee.

Photo Credits

Cover, pp. 1, 3, 7, 16, 18, 19, 26, 27, 31, 39, 49 © www.istockphoto.com/ Steve Mcsweeny; pp. 4–5, 7, 18, 29, 39 (water) © www.istockphoto. com/Michael Jay; pp. 5, 8–9, 30, 44–45, 46–47 Scott Olson/Getty Images; pp. 10, 14, 25, 40–41, 52–53 © AP Images; p. 12 NOAA; pp. 20–21 © www.istockphoto.com/Gytis Mikulicius; pp. 22–23 Sam Cook/KRT/ Newscom; pp. 32–33 ©Syracuse Newspapers/Berry/The Image Works; pp. 34–35 © Alden Pellett/The Image Works; pp. 36, 50 © www. istockphoto.com/Michael Olson; p. 42 © www.istockphoto.com/ Magdalena Marczewska; back cover and interior silhouettes (figures) © www.istockphoto.com/A-Digit, (grass) © www.istockphoto.com/ Makhnach M.

Designer: Nicole Russo; Editor: Bethany Bryan; Photo Researcher: Amy Feinberg

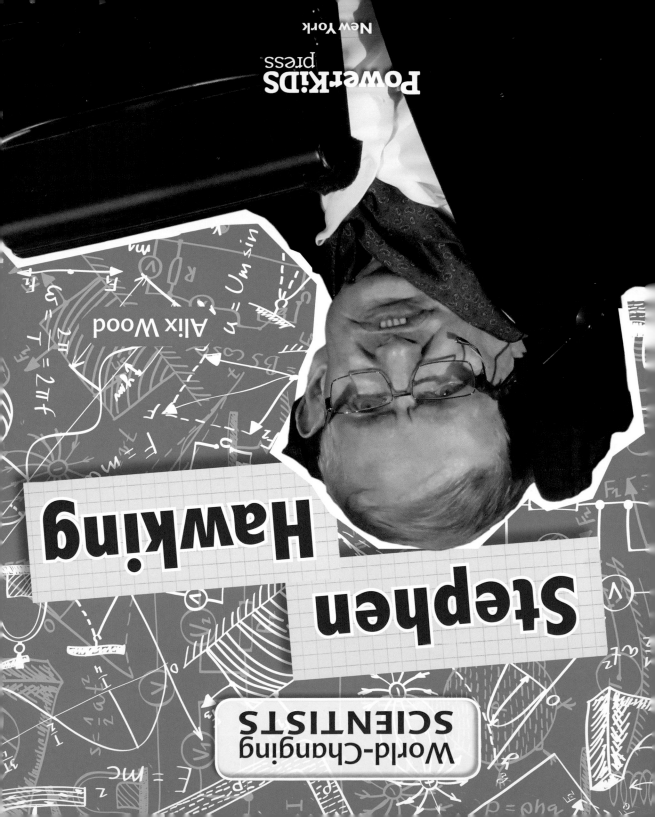

PowerKiDS press
New York

Alix Wood

Stephen Hawking

World-Changing
SCIENTISTS

Published in 2019 by Rosen Publishing
29 East 21st Street, New York, NY 10010

Cataloging-in-Publication Data

Names: Wood, Alix.
Title: Stephen Hawking / Alix Wood.
Description: New York : PowerKids Press, 2019. | Series:
World-changing scientists | Includes glossary and index.
Identifiers: LCCN ISBN 9781538337943 (pbk.) | ISBN 9781538337936
(library bound) | ISBN 9781538337950 (6 pack)
Subjects: LCSH: Hawking, Stephen, 1942---Juvenile literature. |
Physicists--Great Britain--Biography--Juvenile literature. |
Scientists--Great Britain--Biography--Juvenile literature.
Classification: LCC QC16.H33 W64 2019 | DDC 539.092 B--dc23

Adaptations to North American edition © 2019
by Rosen Publishing

Produced for Rosen Publishing by Alix Wood Books
Designed by Alix Wood
Editor: Eloise Macgregor

Consultant: Kevin E. Yates, Fellow of the
                Royal Astronomical Society

Photo credits:
Cover, 1 © Martin Hoscik/Shutterstock; 4 © NASA/StarChild; 6, 8, 9
bottom, 11, 13, 23 © Adobe Stock Images; 9 top © Gary Houston, 10 ©
Andrew Shiva/Wikipedia; 15 © Alain Riazuelo/NASA; 18 © Paul Alers/
NASA; 19 © Steve Jurvetson; 20 © Pete Souza/Whitehouse Photostream;
22, 26, 27 © Alix Wood; 24, 25 © NASA; all other images are in the
public domain

Printed in the United States of America

CPSIA compliance information: Batch #CS18PK: For further information contact Rosen
Publishing, New York, New York at 1-800-542-2595.

Contents

World -Changing Scientist
Dr. Stephen Hawking

Dr. Stephen Hawking was a world-famous British **theoretical physicist** who lived from January 8, 1942 to March 14, 2018. A theoretical physicist is a scientist who uses math to study theories about the universe, such as how it began and how it might change in the future. He was best known for his study of **black holes**. His book *A Brief History of Time* was an international bestseller.

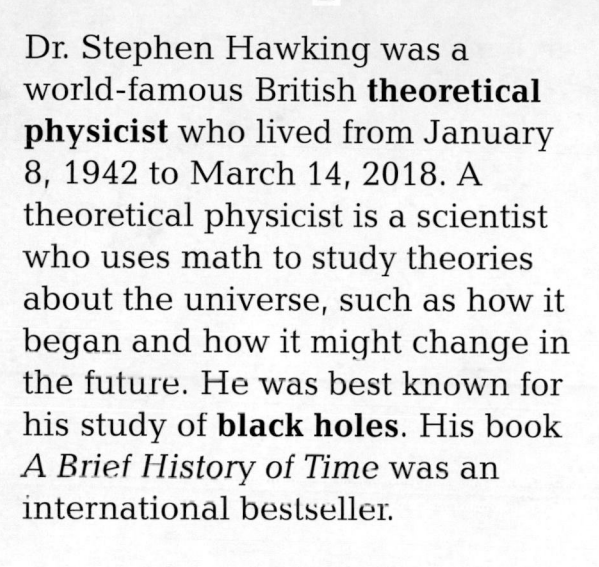

Science Notes

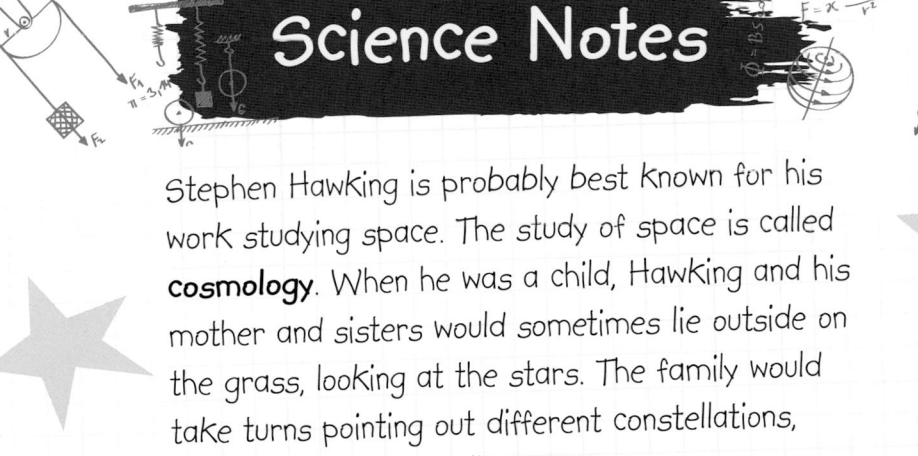

Stephen Hawking is probably best known for his work studying space. The study of space is called **cosmology**. When he was a child, Hawking and his mother and sisters would sometimes lie outside on the grass, looking at the stars. The family would take turns pointing out different constellations, and excitedly watch falling stars.

"All of my life, I have been fascinated by the big questions that face us, and have tried to find scientific answers to them. If, like me, you have looked at the stars, and tried to make sense of what you see, you too have started to wonder what makes the universe exist."

STEPHEN HAWKING

Hawking loved science and math at school. He found physics lessons too easy, so he didn't enjoy them as much as math! He was so good at science he was called Einstein by his friends, after the famous physicist Albert Einstein! Einstein is famous for his **theory of relativity**. Einstein's famous theory helped Hawking during his study of black holes.

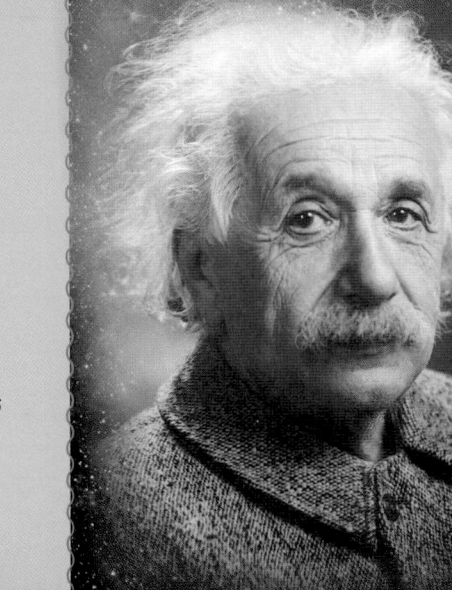

Stephen's Childhood

Stephen William Hawking was born in Oxford, England, on January 8, 1942. This was, coincidentally, the 300th anniversary of the death of another very famous scientist, Galileo. Stephen was born during World War II. His family lived in North London, but the bombing during the war meant it wasn't very safe there. Stephen's parents decided to move to Oxford to have their baby.

Stephen was the eldest of four children. He had two younger sisters, Mary and Philippa, and his parents adopted his younger brother, Edward, when Stephen was 14 years old. His family was clever and a little **eccentric**. His Scottish mother had studied at Oxford University at a time when only a few women went to college. His father also studied at Oxford, and became a medical researcher working with tropical diseases.

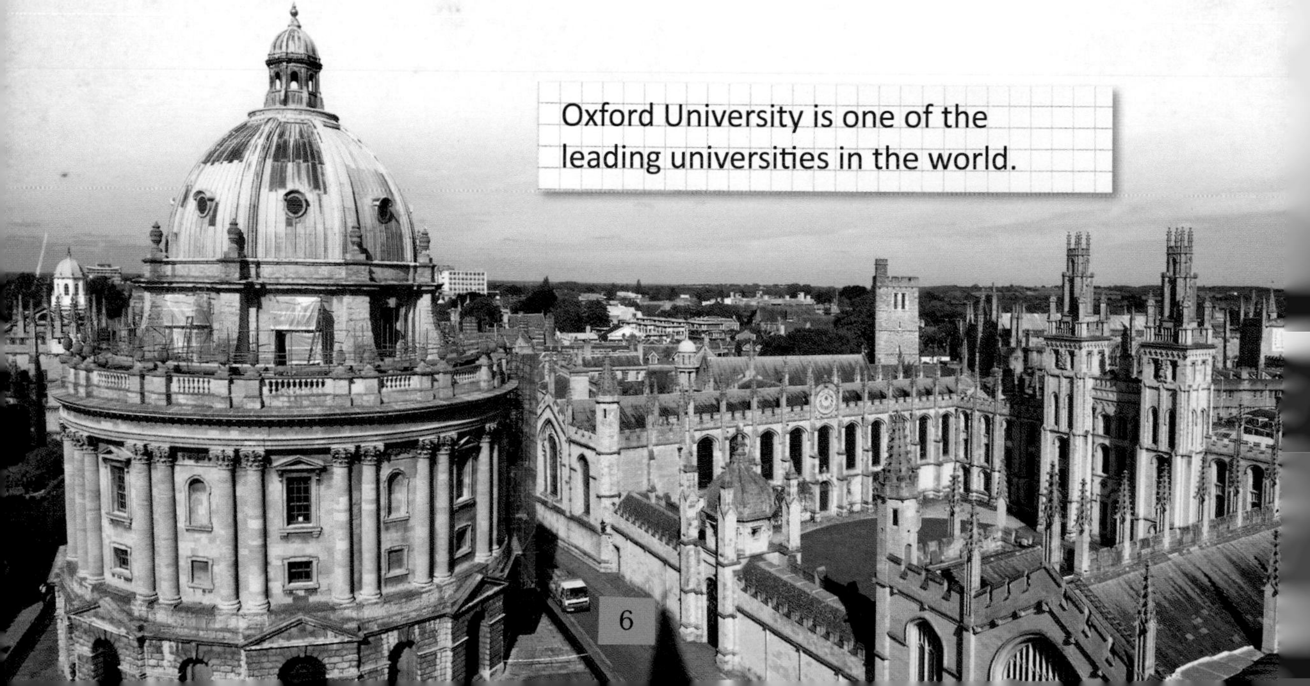

Oxford University is one of the leading universities in the world.

Science Notes

All great science discoveries follow on from the work of scientists that have gone before them. Much of Stephen Hawking's work on the mysteries of space were possible because of the discoveries by scientists such as Galileo.

Who Was Galileo?

Galileo Galilei was an Italian **astronomer**. He was also brilliant at physics, engineering, **philosophy**, and math! He played a big part in the scientific revolution that happened during the seventeenth century. He developed the telescope, and with it discovered four of the moons of the planet Jupiter. They were named the Galilean moons in his honor. Galileo discovered sunspots, and invented an improved military compass.

Galileo's views on the solar system were so ahead of their time that he was put under house arrest for **heresy**!

When Stephen was eight, the family moved to an old three-story home in a town near London, called St Albans. The house needed fixing up and was a bit of a shambles. Friends say that the family often sat in silence at mealtimes, each person intently reading a book. The Hawkings had some unusual hobbies, too. Stephen's father kept bees in the basement, and made his own fireworks in the greenhouse.

The Hawkings' family car was an old black London taxi cab!

Stephen went to St Albans School, a private school full of bright pupils, with a high standard of teaching. His Armenian math teacher, Dick Tahta, helped nurture Stephen's love of mathematics. Together, they built a giant computer out of scrap parts from an old telephone switchboard! Many of Stephen's classmates were very bright. He was not the smartest pupil, and believed himself to be about the middle of his class.

Stephen and his friends liked to build and fly model airplanes. Stephen also invented complicated board games. Friends have said it could take most of the evening to work out the rules before anyone even threw the dice!

St Albans School is one of the oldest schools in the world. It was founded in 948 by Wulsin, the abbot of St Albans Abbey.

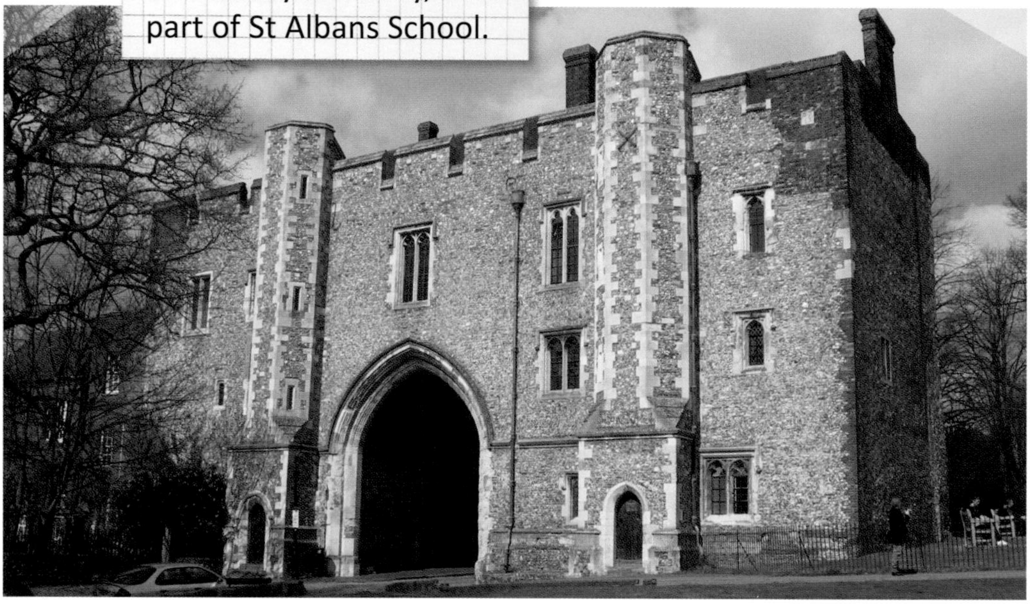

The Abbey Gateway, part of St Albans School.

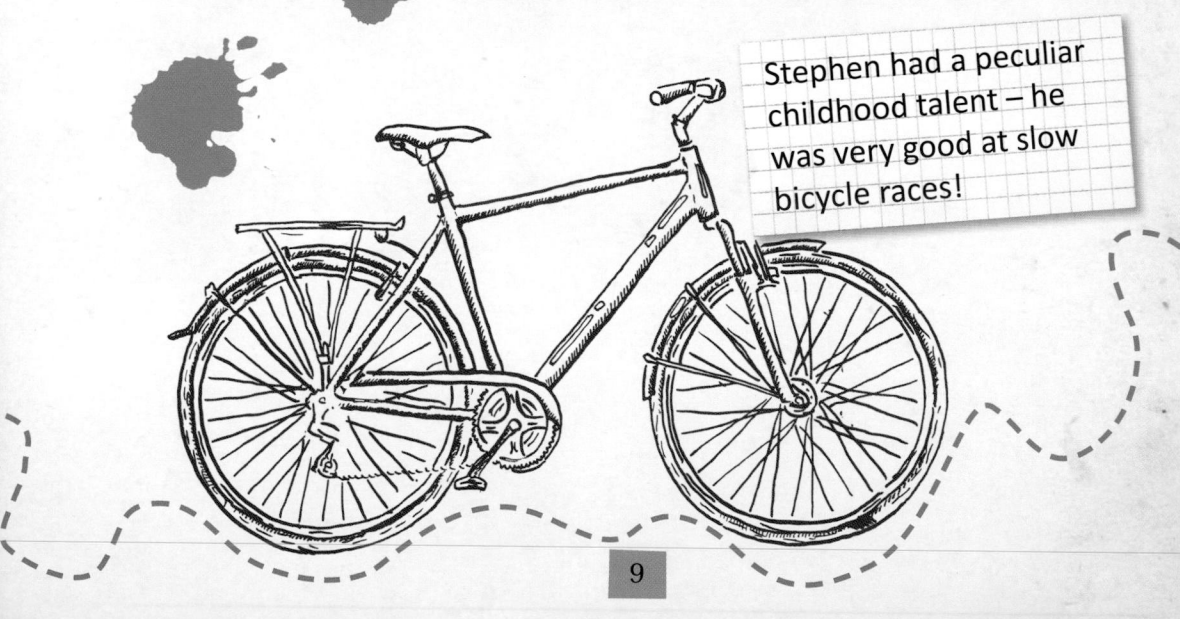

Stephen had a peculiar childhood talent – he was very good at slow bicycle races!

University Days

Stephen Hawking wanted to study math at university, but his father wanted him to study medicine and become a doctor. As a compromise, Hawking applied to go to his father's old college, University College, Oxford. At that time you couldn't study math there, so Hawking chose to study physics instead. When he took the entrance exam, he got a near-perfect score in the physics section! Hawking was awarded a **scholarship**.

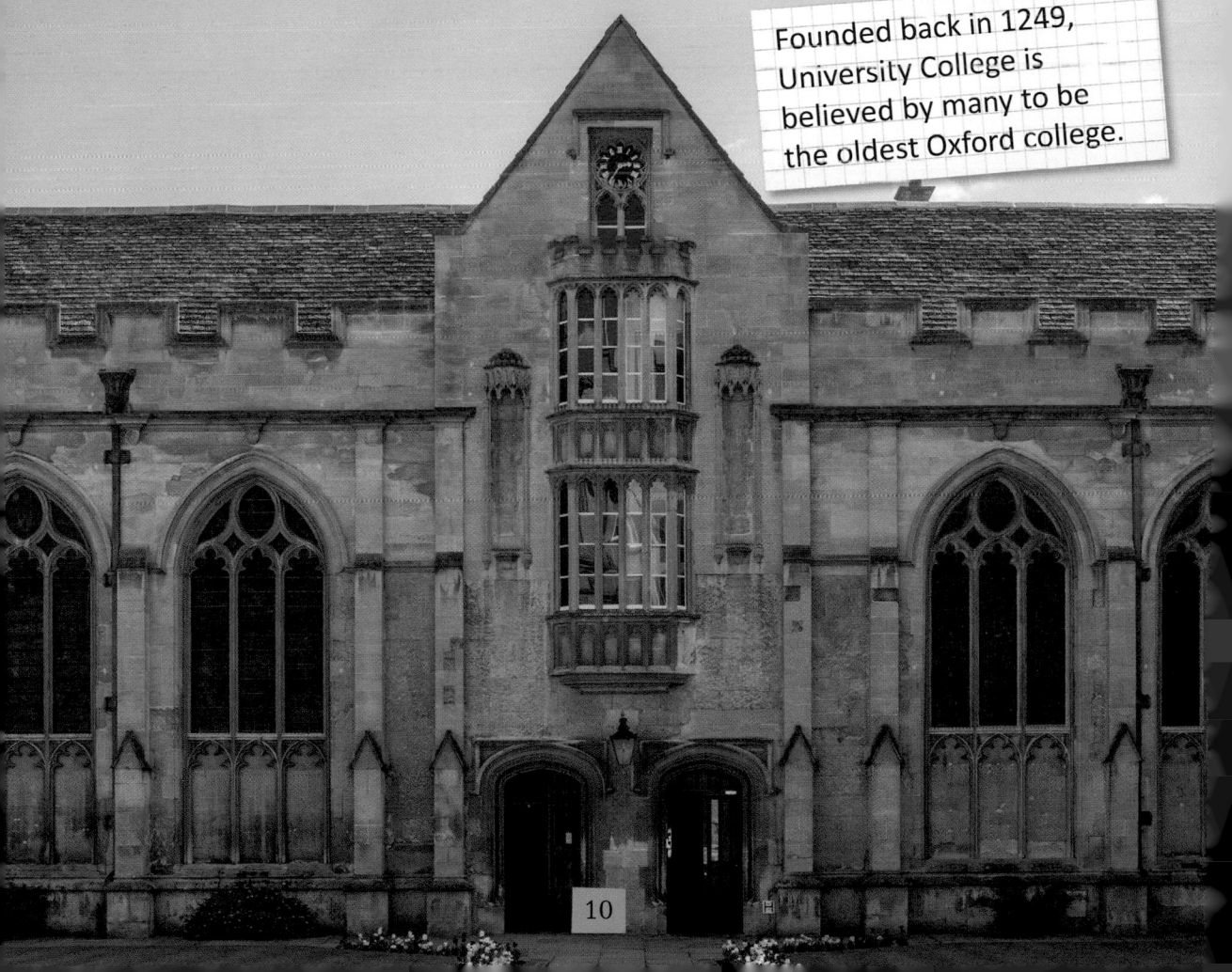

Founded back in 1249, University College is believed by many to be the oldest Oxford college.

Hawking was 17 years old when he went to Oxford, a year younger than most other students. Because of this, Hawking was a little lonely and unhappy during his first year at university. To help meet people and cheer himself up, Hawking joined the rowing team.

The cox sits facing the rowers and shouts out commands. They also help steer the boat by moving the rudder.

Hawking was not a very sporty person. His slight build meant he would never be a great oarsman. However, small men like Hawking are valuable as **coxswains**, or coxes. Coxes don't row. Instead they control the steering and boss the rowers. The lighter the cox, the faster the boat can travel! Rowing is very important and competitive at Oxford. Being a member of the rowing team helped make him popular.

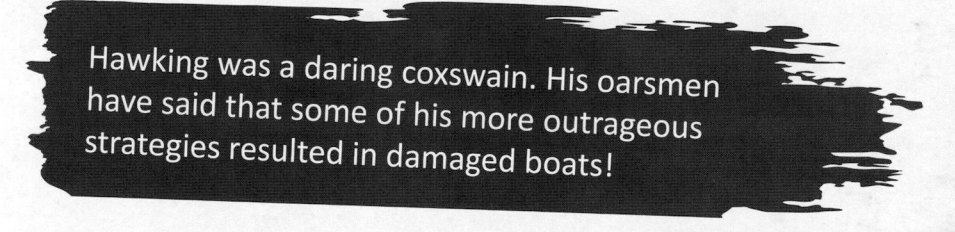

Hawking was a daring coxswain. His oarsmen have said that some of his more outrageous strategies resulted in damaged boats!

In his last year at Oxford, Hawking began to become a little clumsy. It was not taken that seriously. After falling down the stairs, his doctor advised him not to drink beer!

After graduating from Oxford with a first class degree in physics, Hawking went to Trinity Hall, Cambridge University to research **general relativity** and cosmology.

Hawking began to notice that he was becoming more and more clumsy. When he went home at the end of his first term at Cambridge, his mother persuaded him to go to the doctor. He was found to have ALS, also known as motor neurone disease, or Lou Gehrig's disease. His condition quickly got worse. Doctors thought that he would not live long enough to complete his studies at Cambridge.

What is ALS?

ALS is a disease that weakens the nerves and muscles. Stephen Hawking suffered from a rare, slow-progressing form of the disease. The average age to be diagnosed with ALS is 55, but Stephen Hawking was only 21 when he found out he had the illness. The disease gradually paralyzed him over the years. At the end of his life, he used a wheelchair and communicated using a single cheek muscle attached to a speech-generating device. None of this stopped him from living an incredibly productive life. His most important work was done long after the disease took hold.

Despite his condition, Hawking enjoyed this time at Cambridge. He was making progress in his research. He had also fallen in love with Jane Wilde, one of his sister's friends that he met at a New Year's party. He realized that if he only had a few years to live, he needed to quickly work hard to achieve all the things he wanted to do in his life.

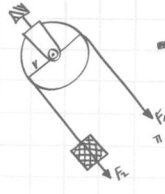

Science Notes

Relativity and the Speed of Light

You may think light doesn't travel at a certain speed, it is just there or not there. Light actually does have a speed, it is just really fast. It travels at an amazing 186,000 miles (299,794 km) a second!

Cosmologists use the speed of light to measure how far away things are in the universe. A light-year is the distance light travels in one year, which is about 5,900,000,000,000 miles (9,500,000,000,000 km). If you switched a light on in space 5,900,000,000,000 miles away, it would take a whole year to see the light from Earth! Some stars we can see at night are so far away that the light we see left them thousands of years ago!

Albert Einstein believed light always traveled at the same speed. But scientist Isaac Newton had discovered that the speed of things could change under different conditions. Surely the same could be true of light? This idea fascinated Hawking. At Cambridge, his essay "Singularities and the Geometry of Space-Time" explored the idea that the speed of light could change. His essay was so good it won a prize that year.

Hawking stayed at Cambridge and was given a fellowship to study black holes at Gonville and Caius College. Hawking worked with a scientist named Roger Penrose at this time. Hawking brought two complicated fields of science together while studying black holes; Einstein's theory of general relativity and **quantum theory**. The theory of general relativity led scientists to realize that black holes might exist. Quantum theory examines how energy and the tiniest particles of matter, smaller than atoms, behave.

Science Notes

What Is a Black Hole?

A black hole forms when a very large star dies and collapses inward, creating a powerful gravitational pull at its center. The force of gravity is so strong that even light is not able to escape. The gravity is strong because the star's matter has been pressed into a tiny, dense space.

Because no light can escape from a black hole, they are invisible. How do we know they are there? Powerful telescopes with special instruments can help scientists observe the behavior of objects close to black holes. Gravity makes objects in space travel around larger objects in a regular pattern, known as an **orbit**. By watching any stars' slight changes in movement, scientists can predict where the strong pull of a black hole may be.

Hawking Radiation

Perhaps Stephen Hawking's most famous discovery was finding that black holes could leak energy and particles into space, now known as Hawking Radiation. In space, tiny particles known as photons exist in pairs—one is matter and the other is **antimatter**. The two particles usually quickly cancel each other out and die. Near a black hole, though, the antimatter may fall into the hole, while the matter escapes. Before Hawking discovered this, scientists believed black holes couldn't get smaller as nothing could escape their gravity. Hawking proved that black holes could get smaller, and could even explode!

An artist's impression of a black hole.

A Brief History of Time

Stephen Hawking wrote several books that help explain cosmology to people who have little or no scientific knowledge. In 1988, Stephen Hawking's book *A Brief History of Time* was published. This book described theories such as the **Big Bang** and black holes in a way that could be easily understood. The book was popular, selling millions of copies, and was translated into many languages.

Hawking began writing *A Brief History of Time* in 1983. He discussed the idea for a popular book on cosmology with Simon Mitton, who was the editor in charge of astronomy books at Cambridge University Press. His first manuscript was full of complicated **equations**. Mitton felt the equations were too off-putting for the average reader Hawking wished to reach.

Hawking was warned that every equation he put in his book would cut his readership by half! He was persuaded to drop all but one equation, Einstein's famous theory of relativity, $E = mc^2$.

$$F = ma$$

$$\pi = 3.14$$

$$E = mc^2$$

$$s = vt$$

$$s = \tfrac{1}{2}at^2$$

$$2yd = d$$

$$n = Um \sin wt$$

$$\phi = BS \cos \alpha$$

$$v = \sqrt{2gh}$$

$$g = 9.8 ms^{-2}$$

$$F = \varkappa \frac{m_1 m_2}{r^2}$$

$$w = \frac{2\pi}{T} = 2\pi f$$

What Is the Big Bang?

The Big Bang theory is an explanation about how the universe began. It is believed that around 13.7 billion years ago all mass, energy, space, and time was packed into an unimaginably hot and dense point, which rapidly expanded. It gradually cooled and matter began to form. A large explosion flung the matter out in all directions. The universe began to expand, and it is still moving outward today.

There is evidence proving the Big Bang theory. Other galaxies are moving away from us, and the further away a galaxy is, the faster it is accelerating. Scientists predicted that a type of heat, known as **afterglow**, would be left over from the Big Bang. Scientists have detected afterglow.

Hawking's health continued to get worse. He went from using crutches to relying on a wheelchair. His speech became difficult to understand. In the 1985, while visiting the CERN laboratory on the border of France and Switzerland, Hawking caught pneumonia. His lifesaving treatment had the side effect of removing what remained of his speaking voice.

Hawking had to communicate by using spelling cards, raising his eyebrows when the correct letter was pointed to. It was frustrating. In 1986, computer programmer Walter Woltosz created a communication system for him. Words and phrases could be selected and spoken by a computerized voice.

Family and Fame

Stephen Hawking had three children, Robert, Lucy, and Timothy, with his wife, Jane. Hawking and Jane divorced in 1991. Hawking later married one of his nurses, Elaine Mason. They divorced in 2006.

Since *A Brief History of Time* was published, Stephen Hawking has gone on to write many books about science for both adults and children. He has co-written several science-themed adventure stories for children with his daughter, Lucy. These include *George's Cosmic Treasure Hunt* and *George and the Big Bang*.

Lucy Hawking presenting her father at a NASA lecture in Washington, D.C.

Stephen Hawking made many TV and movie appearances. He made guest appearances on series from *The Simpsons* to *Star Trek: The Next Generation*. He even did a sketch with Jim Carrey on *Late Night with Conan O'Brien*. In 1992, a documentary named *A Brief History of Time* was made about Hawking's life.

The Theory of Everything

Part of Stephen Hawking's life story was made into a movie, *The Theory of Everything*, released in 2014. Actor Eddie Redmayne played the part of Hawking. When Redmayne won the Best Actor Award at the Oscars for the part, Hawking posted on Facebook, saying, "Well done Eddie, I'm very proud of you." In his acceptance speech, Redmayne dedicated the award to all people living with ALS.

Hawking made a famous funny appearance on the TV show *The Big Bang Theory*, playing himself. In the show, his character finds a mistake in one of the scientist characters' work. His voice was also featured on the Pink Floyd song *Keep Talking*. Stephen Hawking is probably one of the best-known scientists of all time. His appearance and his distinctive computerized voice were instantly recognizable to people, even if they have no interest in physics or cosmology!

Awards and Honors

In recognition of his world-changing scientific work, Stephen Hawking was given many awards, fellowships, and other honors. He was one of the youngest people to be made a Fellow of the Royal Society, at age 32. He was made a Commander of the British Empire in 1982. He turned down a knighthood, saying that he did not like the concept. At the 2016 Pride of Britain Awards, he received the lifetime achievement award for his contribution to science and British culture.

U.S. President Barack Obama meets Stephen and Lucy Hawking at the White House before presenting Hawking with the Presidential Medal of Freedom.

Science Notes

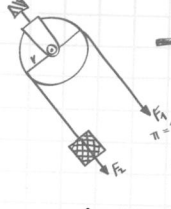

Sir Isaac Newton

Stephen Hawking held the post of Lucasian Professor of Mathematics from 1979 until 2009. It was a great honor. The Lucasian Professor chair began back in 1663. In 1669, the position was held by famous British scientist Sir Isaac Newton. Isaac Newton is one of history's most important scientists. He developed the theory of gravity, the laws of motion, a new type of math known as calculus, and invented the reflecting telescope!

In turn, the Stephen Hawking Medal for Science Communication is an annual award whose winners were chosen by Hawking himself. The awards are given to members of the arts community who help build awareness of science. In 2017, the Medal for Films and Entertainment was awarded to the TV series *The Big Bang Theory*.

Hawking said of his award: "Science communicators put science right at the heart of daily life. Bringing science to the people brings people into science. This matters to me, to you, to the world as a whole."

Solving the Black Hole Paradox

Black holes have an extremely strong gravitational pull, which means that objects close to them are pulled out of their orbits toward them. The **event horizon** is a boundary near the rim of the black hole beyond which nothing can be seen or can escape. This is because the necessary escape speed would have to equal or exceed the speed of light, which is a physical impossibility.

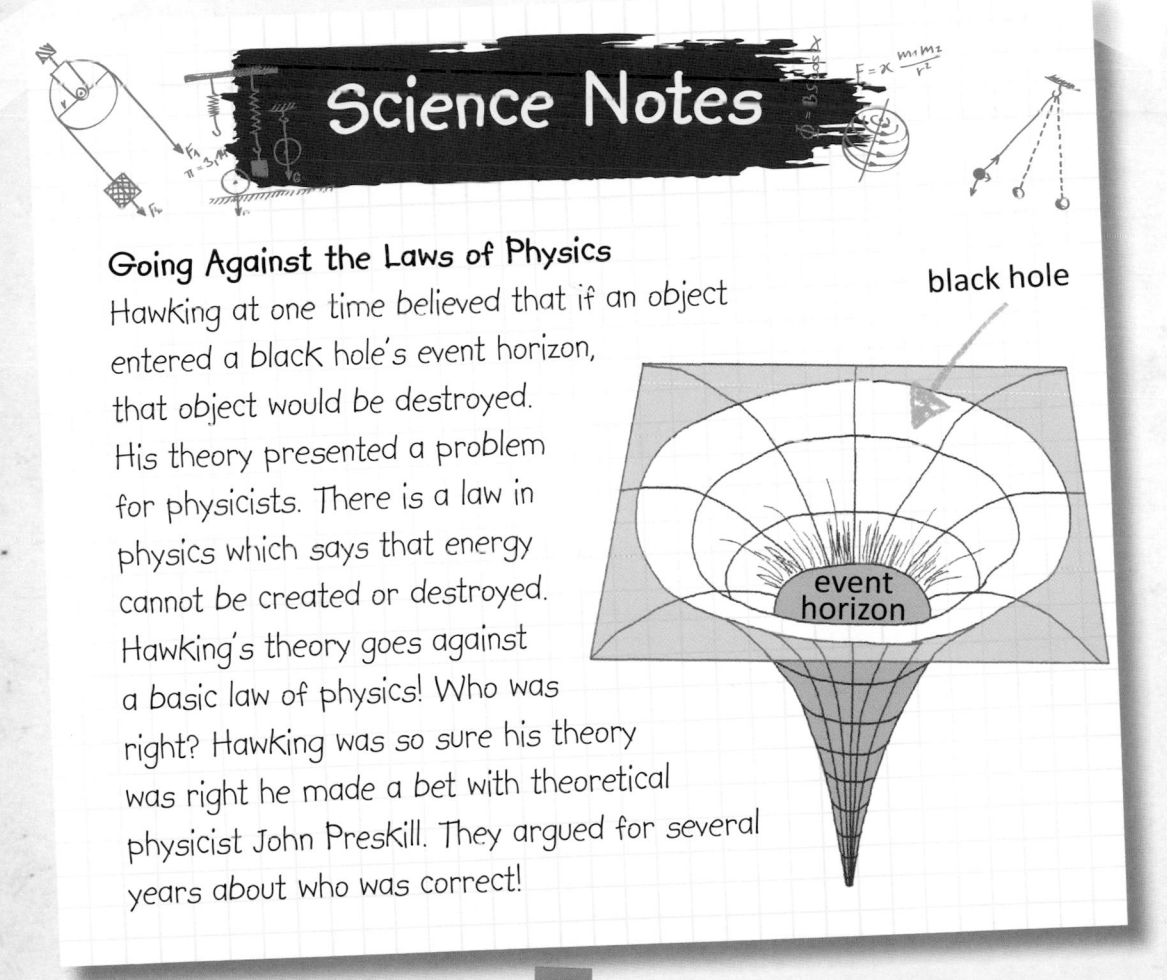

Science Notes

Going Against the Laws of Physics

Hawking at one time believed that if an object entered a black hole's event horizon, that object would be destroyed. His theory presented a problem for physicists. There is a law in physics which says that energy cannot be created or destroyed. Hawking's theory goes against a basic law of physics! Who was right? Hawking was so sure his theory was right he made a bet with theoretical physicist John Preskill. They argued for several years about who was correct!

black hole

event horizon

What Is an Event Horizon?

A black hole behaves in a similar way to a whirlpool in the ocean. When a boat first enters the edge of a whirlpool it would have enough power to escape the pull of its weaker outer edge. However, there is a "point of no return" nearer to the center of the funnel of water where the boat can no longer escape the strength of the whirlpool's pull. That point of no return is like a black hole's event horizon.

Stephen Hawking did some more research into black holes. He began to realize that black holes may actually be more like "gray" holes. That is, they may not destroy everything that enters them, and may allow some matter to escape. He decided that some matter that entered a black hole may possibly be jumbled up rather than destroyed.

In 2004, seven years after Hawking and Preskill's bet, Hawking accepted he had lost. What had the scientists agreed the winner would receive as their prize? The winner got the encyclopedia of their choice! John Preskill chose a copy of *Total Baseball, The Ultimate Baseball Encyclopedia*, which Hawking duly presented to him!

Experiencing Zero Gravity

In 2006, Stephen Hawking was awarded the Copley Medal by the Royal Society for his outstanding contribution to theoretical physics and theoretical cosmology. British astronaut Piers Sellers took the medal with him on a space shuttle mission to the International Space Station.

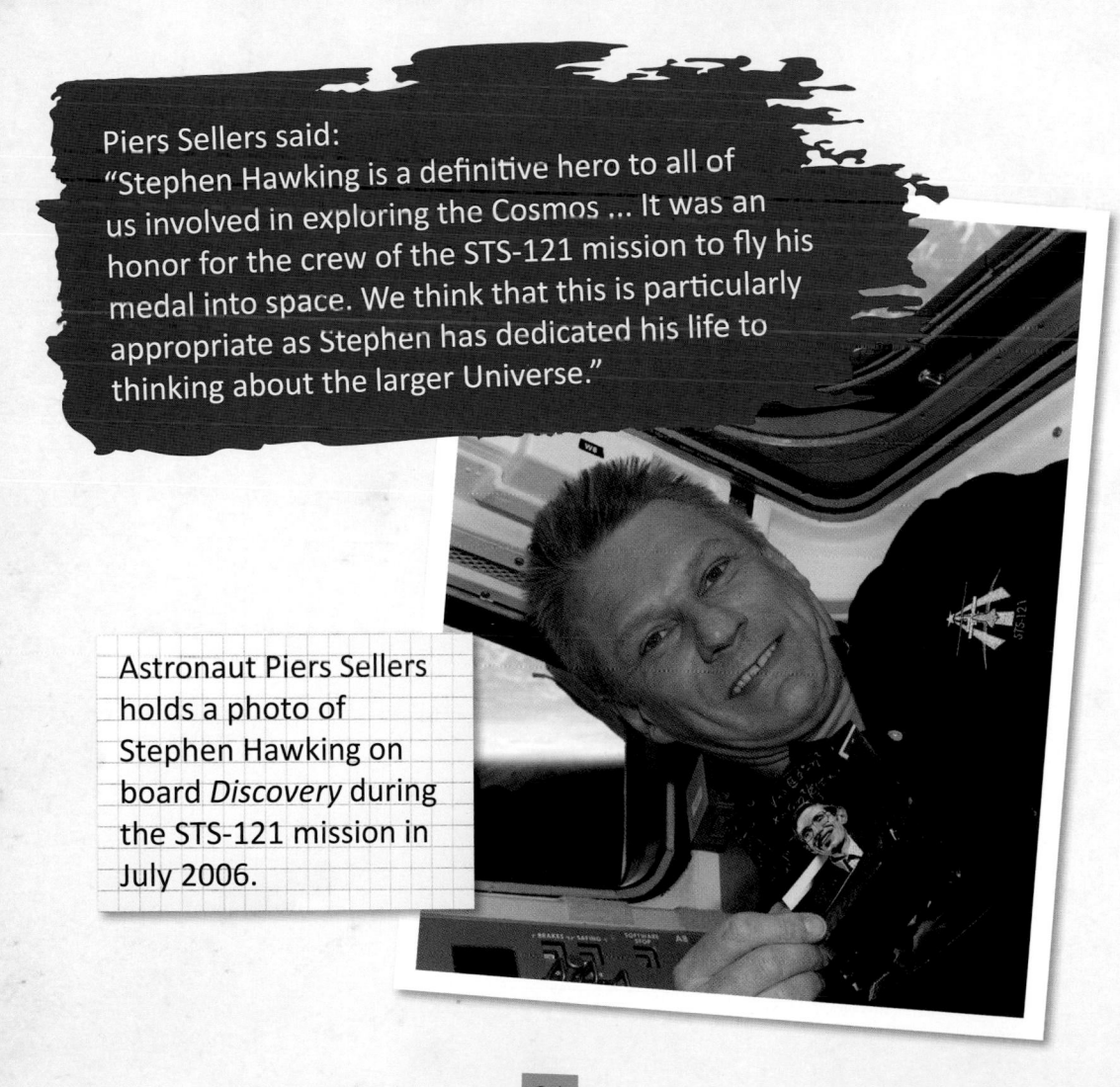

Piers Sellers said:
"Stephen Hawking is a definitive hero to all of us involved in exploring the Cosmos ... It was an honor for the crew of the STS-121 mission to fly his medal into space. We think that this is particularly appropriate as Stephen has dedicated his life to thinking about the larger Universe."

Astronaut Piers Sellers holds a photo of Stephen Hawking on board *Discovery* during the STS-121 mission in July 2006.

In 2007, aged 65, Stephen Hawking experienced a little of what it would be like to travel to space himself. As a passenger on a modified Boeing 727, he experienced floating in zero gravity. The aircraft repeatedly ascends and descends sharply, allowing passengers to experience weightlessness in around 25-second bursts. Hawking was also scheduled to fly to the edge of space as one of Sir Richard Branson's pioneer space tourists. Sadly, he passed away at age 76 on March 14, 2018, before he was able to take this journey.

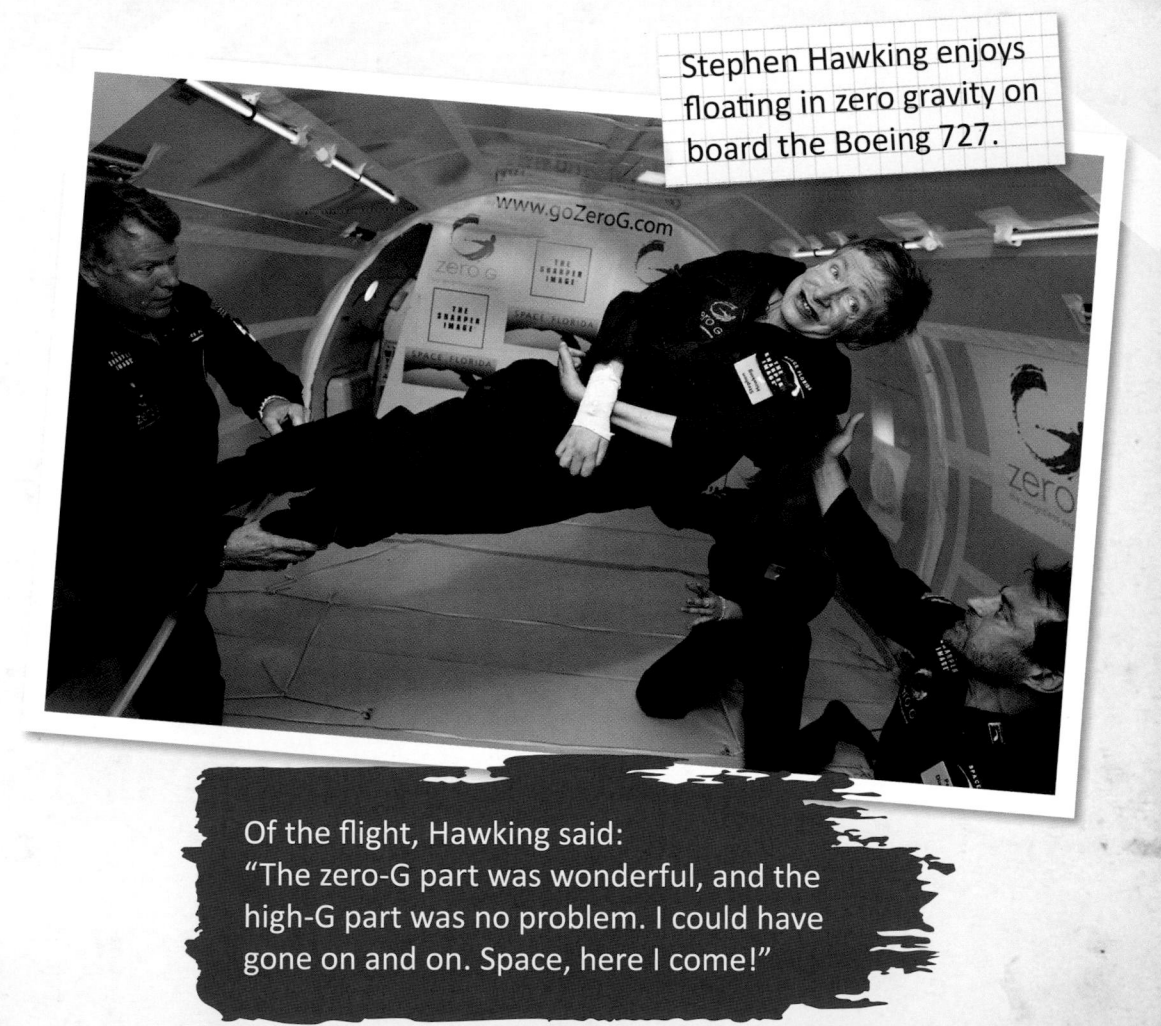

Stephen Hawking enjoys floating in zero gravity on board the Boeing 727.

Of the flight, Hawking said:
"The zero-G part was wonderful, and the high-G part was no problem. I could have gone on and on. Space, here I come!"

Science Project

Exploring gravity and black holes

What happens when you throw a ball straight up into the air? Try it. It will rise for a while, until Earth's gravity makes it start to fall down again. If you could throw a ball hard enough, it could escape Earth's gravity and keep on rising forever. The speed you would need to throw the ball is called the **escape velocity**. Velocity means the speed of something in a given direction. A planet's escape velocity depends on the planet's mass. A massive planet has very strong gravity, so its escape velocity is high. A lighter planet has a lower escape velocity. Also, the closer you are to the planet's center, the higher the escape velocity. Earth's escape velocity is about 25,000 miles per hour (11.2 km per second), while the Moon's is only about 5,300 miles per hour (2.4 km per second).

A black hole has such enormous mass in such a small area that its escape velocity is greater than the speed of light! As nothing can go faster than light, nothing can escape a black hole's gravity, not even a super-fast light beam.

Try this experiment to see how difficult it would be to escape a black hole's gravitational pull.

You Will Need:

- a straw
- some stretchy fabric
- a bucket
- string
- a small, heavy weight
- a much lighter ball
- a marble

1

Place the stretchy fabric over the bucket and tie it securely using the string. The fabric represents space. Place the lighter ball on the fabric. The ball represents a planet with a small mass.

2

Roll your marble so it goes around the small planet. The marble should gradually roll toward it, just like a planet's gravity would pull an object in space.

3

Using a straw, try to blow the marble away from the planet. Can you do it? Swap the light ball for the heavy weight. This represents a black hole.

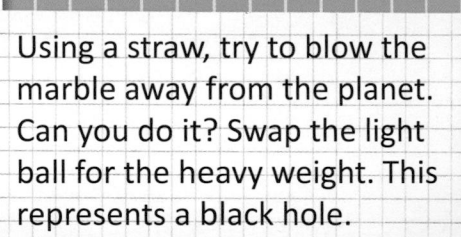

4

Will it be easier or harder to blow the marble and escape a black hole's gravity? Why?

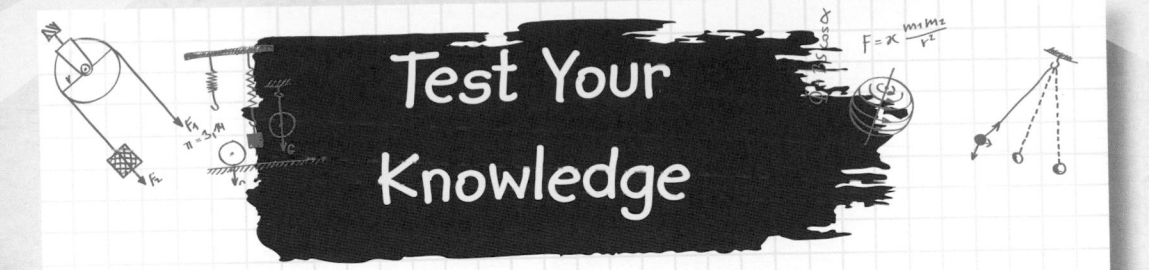

Test Your Knowledge

Test your science knowledge and your memory with this quiz about Stephen Hawking and his work. Can you get them all right? Answers are at the bottom of page 29.

1 Stephen Hawking is best known for his study of
a) engineering b) black holes c) plants

2 What was the title of Hawking's best-selling book?
a) A Brief History of Space
b) A Brief History of Time
c) The Science of Time

3 What is cosmology?
a) the study of space b) business studies c) a magazine

4 What scientist's name did Hawking's school friends call him?

5 What type of transportation did the Hawkings own when Stephen was a boy?
a) a double-decker bus
b) a tandem bicycle
c) a London taxi cab

6 What sport did Hawking take part in while he was at Oxford University?

a) rowing b) soccer c) rugby

7 If you switched a light on in space a light-year away from Earth, how long would it take us on Earth to see the light?

a) a millisecond b) a year c) an hour

8 What do you call a region of space that has such strong gravity that not even light can escape?

a) a dark circle b) a star c) a black hole

9 What is the Big Bang theory?

a) an explanation of how the universe began
b) a theory explaining how we can hear noises in space
c) the reason why comets occur

10 Are other galaxies around us completely still, or constantly moving away from us?

Answers

1. b – black holes; 2. b – A Brief History of Time; 3. a – the study of space; 4. Einstein; 5. c – a London taxi cab; 6. a – rowing; 7. b – a year; 8. c – a black hole; 9. a – an explanation of how the universe began; 10. other galaxies are constantly moving away from us

Glossary

afterglow   Leftover heat from the fireball of the big bang.

antimatter   Each particle of matter has a corresponding antiparticle of antimatter.

astronomer   A scientist who studies the stars, planets, and other natural objects in space.

Big Bang   The explosion believed to have caused the beginning of the universe.

black holes   An invisible region believed to exist in space having a very strong gravitational field and thought to be caused by the collapse of a star.

cosmology   A branch of astronomy that deals with the beginning, structure, and space-time relationships of the universe.

coxswains   People who steer a boat.

eccentric   Acting or thinking in an unusual way.

equations   Written math statements using symbols that show that two values are the same.

escape velocity   The lowest speed that a moving body must have to escape from the field of gravity.

event horizon   The boundary around a black hole beyond which no light or other radiation can escape.

general relativity   The theory that matter causes space to curve.

heresy   An opinion that is opposed to the doctrines of a church.

orbit   To circle around.

philosophy   The study of the basic ideas about knowledge, truth, right and wrong, religion, and the nature and meaning of life.

quantum theory   A theory that describes nature at the smallest scales of energy levels of atoms and subatomic particles.

scholarship   Money given to a student to help pay for further education.

theoretical physicist   Scientists who use math to describe certain aspects of nature.

theory of relativity   The theory that the speed of light is constant for all observers; and observers moving at constant speeds should be subject to the same physical laws.

For More Information

Cornell, Kari. *Theoretical Physicist Stephen Hawking* (Stem Trailblazer Bios). Minneapolis, MN: Lerner Classroom, 2016.

Edwards, Chris. *All About Stephen Hawking* (All About... People). Indianapolis, IN: Blue River Press, 2018.

Hawking, Lucy, and Stephen Hawking. *George's Secret Key to the Universe*. New York, NY: Simon & Schuster Books for Young Readers, 2009.

Newland, Sonya. *Inspirational Lives: Stephen Hawking*. London, UK: Wayland Publishing, 2016.

Websites
Due to the changing nature of Internet links, PowerKids Press has developed an online list of websites related to the subject of this book. This site is updated regularly. Please use this link to access the list:

www.powerkidslinks.com/wcs/hawking

Index